Snappy Style

Paper Decoration Creations

by Jennifer Phillips

CAPSTONE PRESS
a capstone imprint

Table of Contents

Fold it.
Tear it.
Make it.
Display it.

Paper is an amazing, inexpensive material that can easily be transformed into fantastic decorations for your home. There's also a special bonus to making your own decorations—they're one of a kind!

Ready to get started? Start by gathering paper. You can find colorful paper and printed card stock at craft and office supply stores. Recycled papers, such as old sheet music, maps, posters, or wrapping paper are great options too. Next get those craft tools ready. You probably already have basic paper craft tools like scissors, rulers, and craft glue. Any supplies you don't have can be found at most hardware, craft, or office supply stores.

Paper isn't just for scratching messages on. Spruce up your rooms with paper crafts that will impress any visitor.

1. tweezers
2. craft knife
3. spray paint
4. foam brush
5. decoupage glue
6. hole punch
7. slotted quilling tool
8. quilling needle

Newspaper Basket

Snag a copy of the Sunday paper, and weave this unique basket. It's a perfect decoration for a living room, plus it keeps things organized!

6

1. Trim off the newspaper folds so you have single pages.

2. Fold each page into a long strip that is about 1½ inches (4 centimeters) wide.

3. Put two strips side by side on your workspace horizontally. Weave a third strip over and under the middle of the first strips. Glue the third strip in place.

4. Weave three more strips on the left side of the vertical strip. Then weave four strips on the right side of the vertical strip. Make sure the strips are close together. Glue the strips in place.

5. Turn the project so the horizontal strips are vertical. Then weave in six more strips so you have a total of eight in the center. Make sure these are close together too. Glue the strips in place. This will be the bottom of the basket.

6. Fold the leftover stripping up to shape the side frames. It's OK if they don't all stand up on their own. They will later.

7. Glue one paper strip end to a corner along the bottom of one side. Weave the strip horizontally along the bottom, going in and out of the strips you folded up to make the frame. Glue the strip to the frame as you work to keep it from sliding. When you reach a corner, pinch the strips together to make a corner angle.

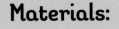

Materials:

at least 22 newspaper pages

glue stick

stapler

wide ribbon

Tip: Newspaper ink will get all over your hands. Wear some old clothes and expect to get a little messy.

When you reach the end of the strip, glue another strip to it and continue weaving until you reach the corner where you started. Trim off any excess paper and glue the ends together.

8. Repeat step 7 two or three more times. Your sides will have three or four rows, depending on how tall you want the basket to be.

9. Fold excess frame strips over so they lay flat on the inside. Staple the top of each top strip. Trim away the extra paper below the staples.

10. Glue ribbon around the basket's top to hide the staples and give the basket a finished look.

Silhouette Tree

Assemble a unique family tree, complete with pets and friends, to decorate your home. A wall makes a spectacular canvas.

1. On the back side of the shelf liner, draw a tree trunk that is 24 inches (61 cm) tall or taller. Then draw branches and leaves in the sizes and shapes you want. Cut out the shapes. Peel off the paper backing and attach your tree to a wall.

2. Cut out the subject of a photo. Cut carefully so you don't lose the little details.

3. Trace the cut photo onto construction paper. Cut out the silhouette.

4. Cut a piece of decorative paper into a fun shape, such as an oval, star, or house. Make this shape large enough that the silhouette can fit on top.

5. On a different piece of paper, cut a larger version of the shape you cut in step 4.

6. Glue the smaller shape to the larger shape. Then glue the silhouette on top.

7. Repeat steps 2–6 to create several other silhouette pictures.

8. Attach the silhouette pictures to the tree with hidden squares of masking tape.

Tip: Choose photos that have fun details, such as wisps of hair, curly tails, or noses. Profile photos work best.

Bookshelf Zoo

Give your book collection some character with these crazy creatures.

1. On a piece of copy paper, draw the animal you want to make. If drawing isn't your thing, do an Internet search for animal templates. Print off one you like.

2. Cut out your drawing or template.

3. Trace the template onto a piece of patterned card stock. Then trace it again on a piece of solid color card stock. Cut out each shape.

4. Glue the patterned animal piece to the solid color animal. Make sure the solid color piece peeks out from behind the patterned piece. This will create a 3D effect.

5. If you wish, enhance a feature on the animal. For example, give it a set of wiggly eyes or paint glitter on a tail.

6. Repeat steps 1–5 for a whole zoo.

Tip: Label the animals with letters from the alphabet or book categories to make organizing your books fun and easy.

Paper Lanterns

Light up a room with this simple but classy
decoration. Fun shapes will dance across
your walls, and you'll dance with enjoyment.

Materials:

8-inch (20-cm) origami
paper squares

craft glue

craft knife

paper punches in fun shapes

string of LED lights

1. Cut two strips 1½ inches (4 cm) wide by 8 inches (20 cm) long from a piece of origami paper.

2. With the pattern side down, form an X with the strips. Glue the strips together where they intersect. The square in the middle of the X will be the bottom of the box.

3. Fold one arm of the X so the outside edge meets the closest edge of the bottom square. Crease the paper so it makes a crisp line. Then fold the square arm over so it lies on top of the bottom square. Crease this fold well too. Unfold.

4. Repeat step 3 with the other three strips.

5. On a protected surface, use a craft knife to cut a small X in the bottom square.

6. Use paper punches to punch out fun designs in each arm of the X. Be careful not to punch holes on the creases.

7. Assemble the box by folding two side strips up on the creases to form a top square. Glue these pieces together. Then fold up the next two sides to join the top square. Glue them all together. Let dry.

8. Repeat steps 1–7 to make enough boxes to cover each light on the string.

9. Before hanging, gently push an LED light through the X in the bottom of each box.

Tip: These boxes can light up any time of year. Use holiday-themed papers to decorate for a special event. Or use papers that coordinate with your room for everyday decor.

Colorful Coverlet

Don't leave your bed out of the decorating fun.
Add a splash of color to any bedroom with this
patchwork paper project.

1. Mix 2 teaspoons (10 mL) of dye with ½ cup (120 mL) of water in a glass or metal bowl. Submerge two paper sheets in the colored water and soak for at least five minutes. Wearing rubber gloves, gently squeeze excess water from the sheets. Place them on newspaper covered with paper towels to dry. Smooth out any wrinkles.

2. Repeat step 1 to dye all the paper sheets. You'll need to dye 20 sheets with one color. Dye six sheets a second color, six sheets a third color, and eight sheets a fourth color.

3. Assemble the dyed blocks according to the pattern shown below. Start with the left column. Put a thin line of hot glue on the long edge of a block. Overlap the long edge of a second block ½ inch (1 cm), and gently press down. Smooth with your finger. Make sure the edges match up and the seams face the same direction as you continue assembling the column. Let dry.

4. Repeat step 3 to create a total of five columns.

5. Attach the columns to each other by running a thin line of hot glue along the edge of a column. Press a second column on top, overlapping ½ inch (1 cm). Let dry well.

6. Take your coverlet to a dry but well-ventilated space. Follow the directions on the can to apply water-resistant sealant.

Materials:

four complementary food dye colors

40 8½x11-inch (22x28-cm) white quilt block foundation non-woven paper sheets

rubber gloves

newspaper and paper towels

hot glue

clear acrylic gloss coating sealant

Tip: This project covers a standard twin bed. If you have a larger bed, double the number of paper sheets and make 10 columns.

Coverlet Pattern

Color 1	Color 1	Color 1	Color 1	Color 1
Color 1	Color 4	Color 2	Color 4	Color 1
Color 2	Color 1	Color 3	Color 1	Color 2
Color 4	Color 3	Color 1	Color 3	Color 4
Color 2	Color 3	Color 1	Color 3	Color 2
Color 4	Color 1	Color 3	Color 1	Color 4
Color 1	Color 4	Color 2	Color 4	Color 1
Color 1	Color 1	Color 1	Color 1	Color 1

Sassy Sachet

Don't just make your place look good. Make it smell good too! You'll actually use a common kitchen paper product to make these perfect pillows.

food dye colors or tea bag

flat bottom (basket style)
coffee filters

paper towels

stencils

thin tipped markers

glue stick

potpourri

1. Mix at least 6 drops of dye with ¼ cup (60 mL) of water in a bowl. For an earthy brown dye, use the tea bag to brew a mug of tea. Let it completely cool, and then pour ¼ cup (60 mL) into a bowl.

2. Flatten a coffee filter so it is a large round circle. Soak it in the dye for at least five minutes.

3. Carefully squeeze the excess water from the filter. Spread the filter on paper towels to dry. They will take a couple of hours to dry.

4. Fold two sides of the filter so they touch in the middle. Fold up the bottom half and then fold down the top half to form flaps of an envelope.

5. Unfold the flaps and turn the filter over. The fold lines show what will be the front of the envelope.

6. On a protected surface, stencil a pattern on the front of the envelope. The markers will bleed through a bit.

7. Turn the envelope back over, refold the sides and bottom flaps. Glue the bottom to the sides. Fill the envelope with potpourri. Glue down the top flap.

8. Repeat steps 1–7 to make as many sachets as you want.

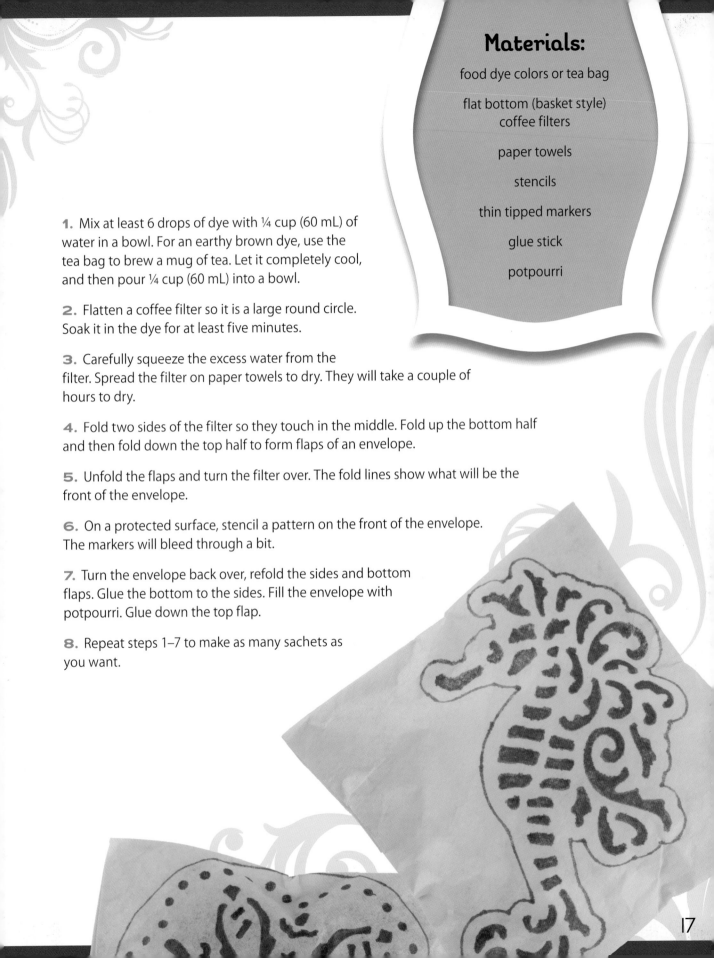

Crafty Creatures

Make your friends hoot and roar with laughter with these silly decorations. And you can store treasures in the jars hidden underneath.

1. Cut a strip of decorative paper 3 inches (8 cm) tall and 9 inches (23 cm) wide. Brush glue on a jar. Wrap the paper around the jar so the top edge is flush against the jar's bottom lip. Hold the paper in place to dry. Repeat with an orange strip of paper and the second jar.

2. Cut a strip of patterned paper 3 inches (8 cm) tall and 10 inches (25 cm) wide. Fold the strip in half, patterned side facing out. Fold each side of the strip inward toward the center fold. Wrap the strip around the top of the blue jar. One fold should face the front and the other folds will be on either side. Glue the back edges together to fit snuggly around the jar. Repeat with orange paper to make the lion's head.

3. Cut two 3½x1-inch (9x2.5-cm) strips and two 4½x1-inch (11x2.5-cm) strips from orange paper. Glue these strips together to make a frame with the longer strips on the top and bottom. Snip a ragged fringe around the outside edges of the frame. Glue the mane to the lion's head.

4. Use a stencil to draw two small ovals on a piece of white paper. Cut out the shapes. Cut out whiskers and a mouth from black paper. Punch out five small circles from the black paper too. Then cut out a nose shape from red paper.

5. Glue the ovals to the lion's face as eyes. Use black circles to create pupils. Glue on the other facial features too. Glue the other black circles to the body like buttons.

6. For the owl, cut two chunky rectangles from black paper. Snip the rectangles into strips for the wings. Cut a rectangle with one pointy end from patterned paper for a necktie. Cut out two small circles from white paper. Cut two half circles and one triangle from orange paper. Punch out two small circles from black paper.

Materials:

decorative paper in several colors, including orange, white, black, and red

foam brush

craft glue

2 half-pint jelly jars

shape stencils

paper hole punch

7. Glue the white circles to the owl as eyes. Use the black circles to create pupils. Glue the orange half circles on top of the white circles as eyelids. Fold the triangle in half. Align the crease with the crease in the head and glue in place. Glue on the wings and necktie too.

8. Cut out four large ovals from orange paper. Glue two ovals to the bottom of each jar as feet.

Letter Lineup

Showcase your personality with cardboard letters featuring papers you love. Try using unusual papers such as maps, photographs, comics, animal prints, or old homework. Make these letters spell YOU!

Materials:

several pieces of thick corrugated cardboard

craft knife

craft glue

decorative papers in a variety of prints and colors

glue stick

foam brush

decoupage glue

1. Using a word processing program, type the letter you want to make. Enlarge the font so the letter fills the whole page. Print it, then cut out your letter. This is your template.

2. Trace the template onto at least two pieces of cardboard. The more cardboard pieces you use, the thicker your finished project will be.

3. Lay one cardboard piece on a protected surface. Use a craft knife to cut out the letter. Repeat with the other cardboard pieces.

4. Stack the letters, using craft glue between each piece to keep them together.

5. Trace your template on a piece of decorative paper. Then turn the template over, and trace it on another piece of decorative paper. Cut out both letters.

6. Use the glue stick to attach the decorative paper to the front and back of the cardboard letter stack.

7. Measure the side width of your letter and the length around the letter edges. Cut out strips of decorative paper in these dimensions. To make this step easier, cut short strips and overlap the edges as you wind around the letter. Attach the strips with the glue stick.

8. Brush decoupage glue over the entire letter for a finished look. Let dry.

9. Repeat steps 1–8 to make as many letters as you need.

Tip: When cutting the cardboard, start with light cuts to make an outline. Then apply more pressure to cut through the layers.

Dot Art

Dot your room with a colorful display. Papers punched into tiny circles can make a surprising decoration when pieced together one by one.

8½x11-inch (22x28-cm) sheet of white card stock

double-sided reusable cling sheets

paper dots of assorted colors

tweezers

picture frame

1. Lightly sketch the picture you want to make on the card stock. It might help to sketch the drawing on copy paper first to avoid too many errors on the card stock.

2. Attach cling sheets to the card stock, filling the whole page. Trim away anything that hangs over the edge of the card stock.

3. Organize the paper dots into color piles.

4. Remove the clear protective film from the tops of the cling sheets. Start creating your picture on the sticky surface one dot at a time. Fill the entire paper so only small portions of the card stock shows through. If you make a mistake, simply use tweezers to move the dots as needed.

5. When you're done, frame your artwork for display.

Tip: Tired of your picture? No problem. Just remove the dots from the adhesive surface and wipe it with a damp cloth. Let the surface dry before starting over.

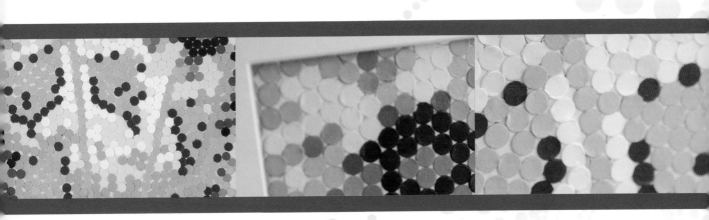

Picture Perfect Lamp

Take a lamp from plain to perfect just by adding paper!
Use papers you love, and let your style shine through.

Materials:

any paper you love, such as sheet music, magazines, maps, or posters

flat-sided lamp shade

glue stick

foam brush

decoupage glue

1. Cut shapes out of your papers. You could cut images from magazines, music note shapes from sheet music, or funky shapes from funky paper.

2. Decide how to arrange your images or shapes on the lamp shade. Once you're certain of the design, use the glue stick to attach the pictures.

3. Carefully brush decoupage glue over the entire lamp shade. Let dry. Then apply a second coat and let dry.

Tip: Look for bargain lamp shades at your local thrift store or garage sales. Just make sure they're in good shape, and clean them when you get home.

Stacked Jewelry Box Tree

Keep your jewelry organized
and decorate your room at
the same time with these
decorated paper boxes.

1. In a well-ventilated area, spray paint three of the boxes inside and out. Also paint the paper mache box. Let dry. Keep the other three boxes and the lid white.

2. Punch paper circles from decorative papers. You probably need at least 70 circles.

3. Use the glue stick to attach dots to all six jewelry boxes and the lid. You can put them in straight rows or mix it up. It's up to you!

4. Brush decoupage glue over all of the jewelry boxes inside and out. Let them dry.

5. Working on a protected surface, use a craft knife to make two ½-inch (1-cm) cuts in the bottom of each box. Make the cuts in an X near the middle of one of the long edges.

6. Turn the paper mache box upside down. Cut a similar X in the center of this box.

7. Slide the boxes onto the dowel through the Xs, and arrange them as you like.

8. Push the bottom end of the dowel into the X in the paper mache box. Fill around the dowel with craft glue to keep it in place. Let dry.

9. Use the craft knife to cut a small X in the middle of the lid. Brush craft glue on the bottom of the button, and gently push the shank through the X so the button sits against the lid. Let dry.

10. Set the lid on top of the jewelry box tree.

Materials:

glossy craft spray paint

6 2x3-inch (5x8-cm) white cardboard jewelry boxes and one lid

4-inch (10-cm) square paper mache box

paper hole punch

decorative paper

glue stick

foam brush

glossy decoupage glue

craft knife

³⁄₁₆x9-inch (.5x23-cm) wooden dowel

craft glue

large button with shank

Garland Wind Chime

Fill your home with music, or at least a few bells. These pretty heart chimes are a decoration that will be music to your ears.

1. Cut five strips, each 1½ inches (4 cm) wide, from wrapping paper. Make two strips 10 inches (25 cm) long, two strips 8 inches (20 cm) long, and one strip 6¾ inches (17 cm) long.

2. Punch a hole about ½ inch (1 cm) from one short edge of the shortest strip.

3. Lay the short strip on your work space, punched hole at the top. Lay an 8-inch (20-cm) strip on top of the short strip with the bottom edges aligned. Glue the bottom edges together.

4. Bend the top edge of the longer strip down into a half heart shape. Glue the edge to the short strip 1½ inches (4 cm) below the hole.

5. Align the bottom edge of a 10-inch (25-cm) strip with the bottom of the heart half. Glue the edges together. Bend the strip around the first heart half to make a second heart half. Tuck the top edge between the short strip and the first heart half, and glue in place.

6. Repeat steps 3–5 on the other side of the short strip.

7. Punch a hole through the glued bottom edges about ½ inch (1 cm) from the edge.

8. Put the open end of a paper clip through the back hook of each bell. Push the bells around the clip to secure. Thread the paper clip through the bottom hole.

9. Thread a paper clip through the top hole. Pull a length of ribbon through the paper clip to create a hanger.

Materials:

reversible wrapping paper

glue stick

paper hole punch

colored paper clips

three small bells

thin ribbon

ed Paper
dle Sleeve

t, warm glow to any
this beautiful glowing
n. Quilled paper designs
around a flameless candle
st the spark you need.

1. Cut wax paper so it will wrap around the candle like a sleeve that fits snugly but can be slipped on and off. Add 2 inches (5 cm) to the height so the paper will be taller than the candle.

2. Insert a quilling strip into the slotted quilling tool. Hold the tool with your dominant hand, and rest the tool on your other hand's forefinger. Roll the tool to quill the paper. When you get to the end, hold the rolled strip securely using your thumb and middle finger. Push the paper roll off the tool.

3. Using the quilling needle, apply glue to the rolled paper end. Press and hold until secure.

4. Repeat steps 2–3 to create several rolled strips. Be creative with the shapes, using the quilling techniques below.

5. Lay the cut wax paper on a table and position your shapes. Pour a bit of glue onto a piece of scratch paper. Grab a quilled shape with tweezers and gently dip the bottom edges in the glue. Set the shape on the paper, and hold it down with your finger until the glue sets. Repeat with all the shapes.

6. Tape the seams of the sleeve together once your design is finished. Slip the sleeve over the candle.

Quilling Techniques

Glue together different colored strips before quilling to create larger shapes of more than one color.

Cut the paper strips shorter to create smaller shapes.

To create more openness within a shape, roll the paper strip tightly. Then loosen up your fingers a bit to get the look you want before gluing down the edge.

To create a square, roll the paper strip into a circle. Then use both hands to pinch all sides inward at the same time.

To create a leaf, roll the paper strip into a circle. Then pinch two ends at the same time.

To create a teardrop shape, roll the paper strip into a circle and pinch one end.

Materials:

wax paper

flameless candle

quilling paper strips

slotted quilling tool

quilling needle

craft glue

tweezers

double-stick tape

Read More

Cho, Minhee and Truman Cho. *Paper + Craft: 25 Charming Gifts, Accents, and Accessories to Make from Paper*. San Francisco: Chronicle Books, 2010.

Phillips, Jennifer. *Adorable Accessories: Paper Creations to Wear*. Paper Creations. North Mankato, Minn.: Capstone Press, 2013.

Youngs, Clare. *Decorating with Papercraft: 25 Fresh and Eco-Friendly Projects for the Home*. Newtown, Conn.: Taunton Press, 2010.

Internet Sites

FactHound offers a safe, fun way to find Internet sites related to this book. All of the sites on FactHound have been researched by our staff.

Here's all you do:

Visit *www.facthound.com*

Type in this code: 9781620650424

Super-cool stuff! Check out projects, games and lots more at **www.capstonekids.com**

Author Bio

Children's author Jennifer Phillips dabbles in all things crafty. A southern Illinois native, Jennifer now calls Seattle home. She likes to write about artists and crafting when not working on her own projects. A member of the Society of Children's Book Writers and Illustrators, her children's work includes articles in *Highlights for Children, Learning through History,* and *Kiki* magazines and several books.

Snap Books are published by Capstone Press,
1710 Roe Crest Drive, North Mankato, Minnesota 56003.
www.capstonepub.com

Library of Congress Cataloging-in-Publication Data
Phillips, Jennifer, 1962–
 Snappy style : paper decoration creations / by Jennifer Phillips.
 p. cm.—(Snap books. Paper creations)
 Includes bibliographical references and index.
 Summary: "Step-by-step instructions teach readers how to
create decorations with paper"—Provided by publisher.
 ISBN 978-1-62065-042-4 (library binding)
 ISBN 978-1-4765-1802-2 (eBook PDF)
 1. Paper work—Juvenile literature. I. Title.
 TT870.P494 2013
 745.54—dc23   2012020247

Editor: **Jennifer Besel**
Designer: **Tracy Davies McCabe**
Project and Photo Stylist: **Brent Bentrott**
Project Production: **Taylor Olson**
Prop Preparation: **Sarah Schuette**
Scheduler: **Marcy Morin**

Photo Credits:
All photos by Capstone Studio/Karon Dubke

Artistic Effects:
Shutterstock: fanny71, HAKKI ARSLAN,
Itana, jojof, Labetskiy Alexandr Alexandrovich,
Lichtmeister, mama-art, Marina Koven, Nils Z,
Polina Katritch, vector-RGB

Printed in the United States of America in
North Mankato, Minnesota.
092012   006933CGS13